NEW EDITION

The Complete Keyboard Player Songbook 3

Published by
Wise Publications
14-15 Berners Street,
London W1T 3LJ, UK.

Exclusive Distributors:
Music Sales Limited
Distribution Centre, Newmarket Road,
Bury St Edmunds, Suffolk IP33 3YB, UK.
Music Sales Pty Limited
Units 3-4, 17 Willfox Street, Condell Park
NSW 2200, Australia.

Order No. AM1008238
ISBN 978-1-78305-430-5

This book © Copyright 2014 Wise Publications,
a division of Music Sales Limited.

Edited by Jenni Norey.
Music processed by Paul Ewers Music Design.

Printed in the EU.

Your Guarantee of Quality
As publishers, we strive to produce every book to the
highest commercial standards.
This book has been carefully designed to minimise awkward
page turns and to make playing from it a real pleasure.
Particular care has been given to specifying acid-free, neutral-sized paper
made from pulps which have not been elemental chlorine bleached.
This pulp is from farmed sustainable forests and was
produced with special regard for the environment.
Throughout, the printing and binding have been planned to
ensure a sturdy, attractive publication which should give years of enjoyment.
If your copy fails to meet our high standards,
please inform us and we will gladly replace it.

www.musicsales.com

Wise Publications
part of The Music Sales Group
London/New York/Paris/Sydney/Copenhagen/Berlin/Madrid/Hong Kong/Tokyo

Beautiful

Words & Music by Linda Perry

Voice: **Alto Saxophone**
Rhythm: **Slow Rock**
Tempo: ♩ = 76

Ev - 'ry day___ is so won - der - ful, then sud - den-

-ly it's hard to breathe.

Now and then___ I get in - se - cure from all the

pain, I'm so a - shamed.

I am beau-ti-ful,_____ no mat-ter what_ they say._____

Words can't bring me_____ down._____

I am beau-ti-ful,_____ in ev-'ry sin-gle way._____ Yes,

words can't bring me_____ down._____ Oh,_____ no._____

So don't you bring me down_____ to - day.

Blue Moon

Words by Lorenz Hart
Music by Richard Rodgers

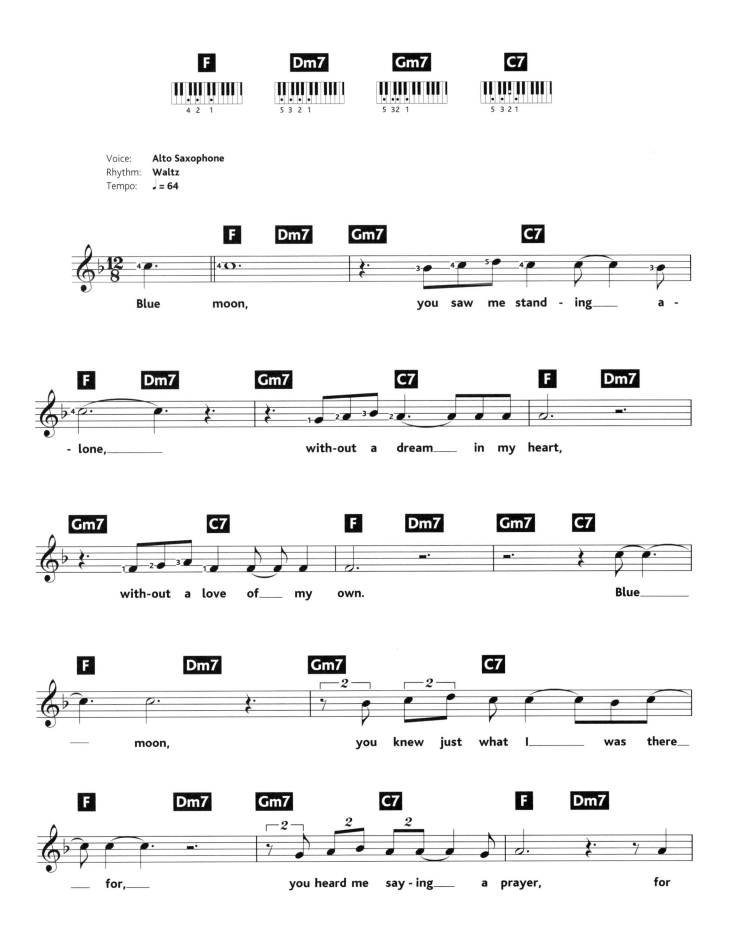

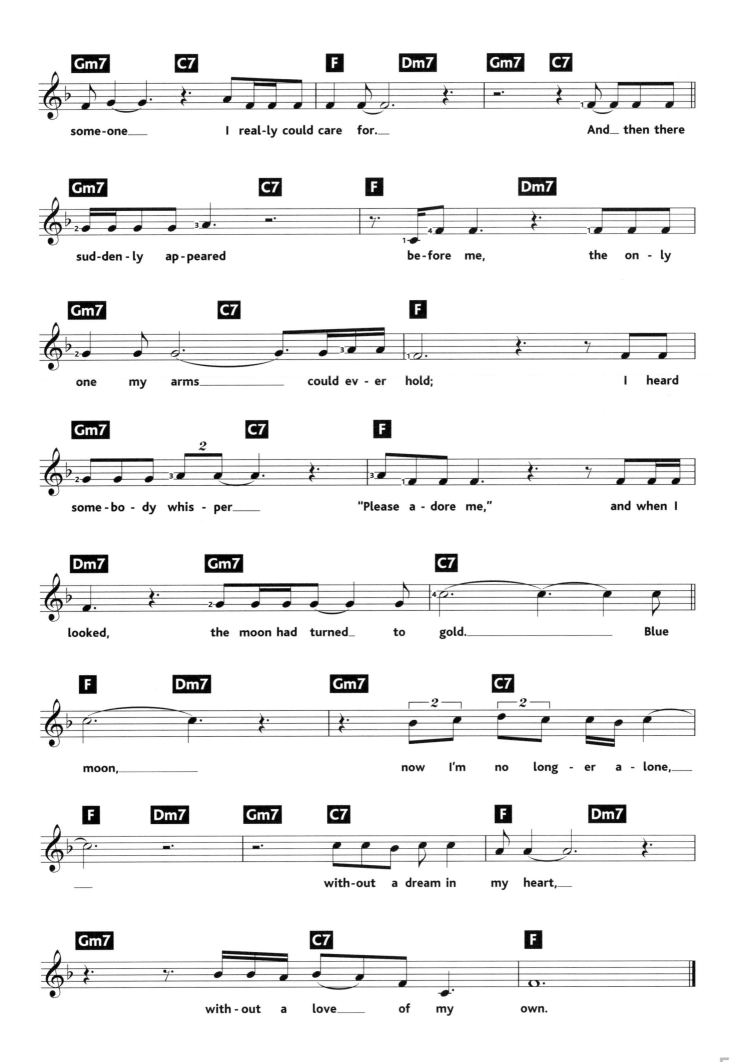

Daisy Bell

Words & Music by Harry Dacre

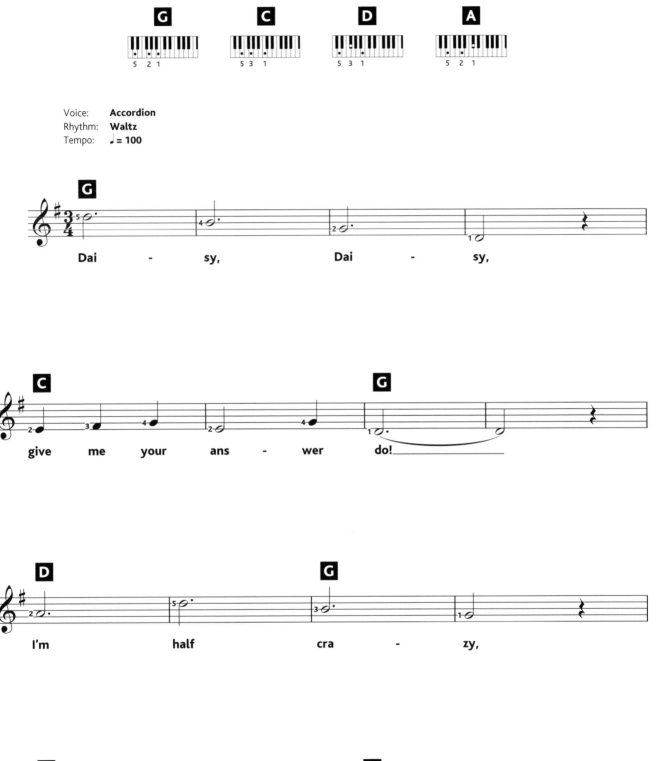

Voice: **Accordion**
Rhythm: **Waltz**
Tempo: ♩ = 100

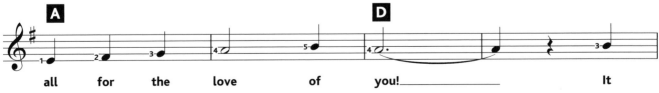

won't be a sty - lish mar - riage, _____ I

can't af - ford a car - riage, _____ but

you'll look sweet on the seat of a

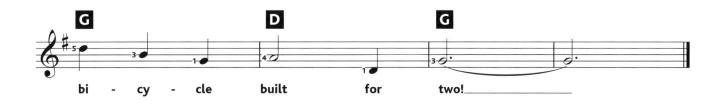

bi - cy - cle built for two! _____

Footloose

Words & Music by Kenny Loggins & Dean Pitchford

Voice: **Electric Guitar**
Rhythm: **Rock & Roll**
Tempo: ♩ = 168

Been work - ing_____ so hard. I'm punch - ing

my_____ card. Eight hours for what?

Oh, tell me what I got. I've got this

feel - ing_____ that time's just hold - ing_____ me down.

I'll hit the

ceil - ing_____ or else I'll tear up this town._____

D

_____ To - night I got - ta cut

G   **C**

loose, foot - loose, kick_____ off your Sun - day

G   **C**

shoes. Please Lou - ise, pull me off_____ of my

G

knees. Jack, get back. Come

C   **G**

_____ on be - fore we crack. Lose your

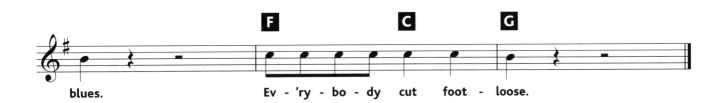

F   **C**   **G**

blues. Ev - 'ry - bo - dy cut foot - loose.

Hallelujah

Words & Music by Leonard Cohen

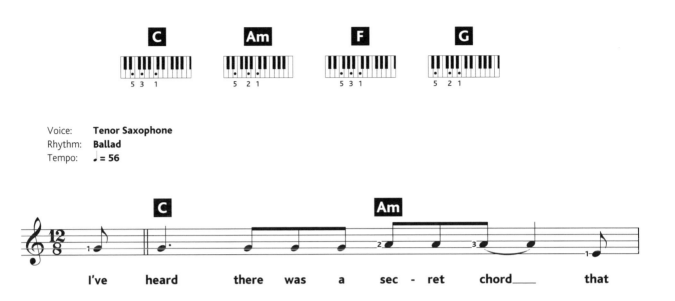

Voice: **Tenor Saxophone**
Rhythm: **Ballad**
Tempo: ♩ = 56

I've heard there was a sec - ret chord____ that

Da - vid played,____ and it pleased the Lord. But

you don't real - ly care for mu - sic, do you? It

goes like this: the fourth, the fifth, the min - or fall, the maj - or lift; the

baf - fled king com - pos - ing Hal - le - lu - jah.___ Hal - le -

-lu - jah, Hal - le - lu - jah, Hal - le -

-lu - jah, Hal - le - lu - jah.

He Ain't Heavy, He's My Brother

Words & Music by Bob Russell & Robert William Scott

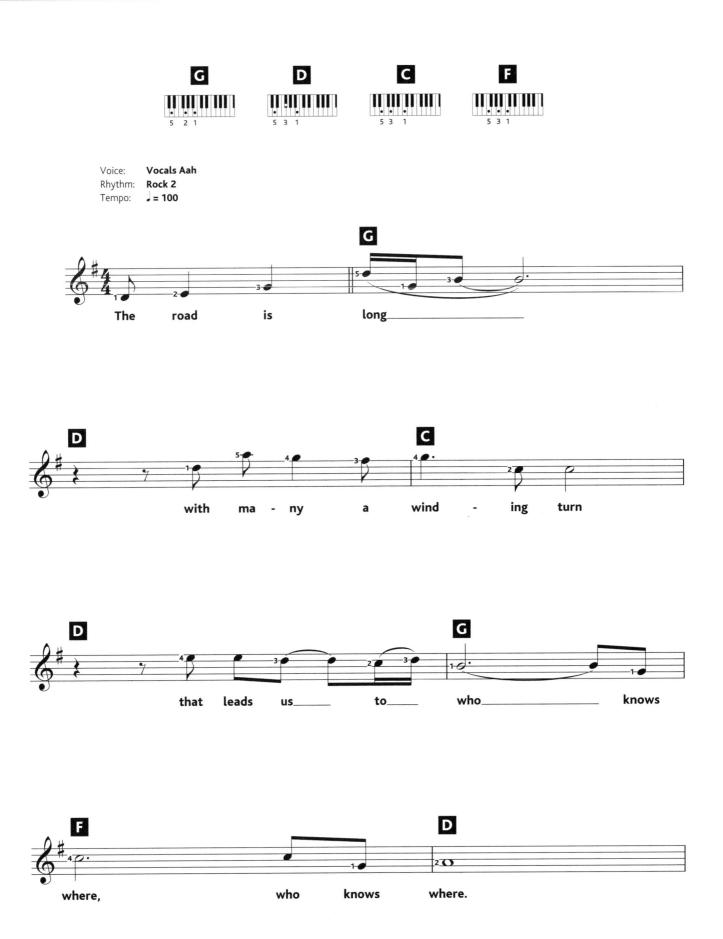

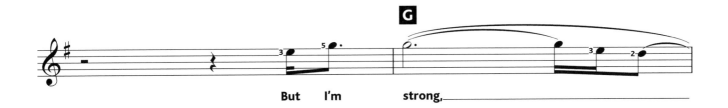

But I'm strong,_____

_____ strong e - nough to car - - ry

him.   He ain't hea - vy,

he's my bro - ther._____

I Am A Rock

Words & Music by Paul Simon

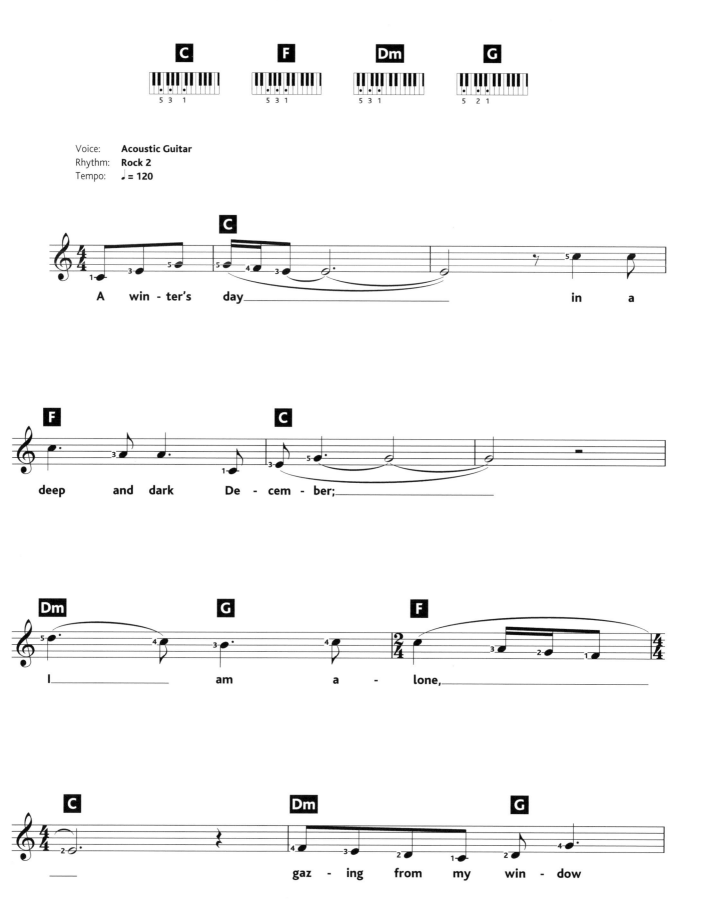

to the streets be - low on a fresh - ly fall - en si - lent shroud of

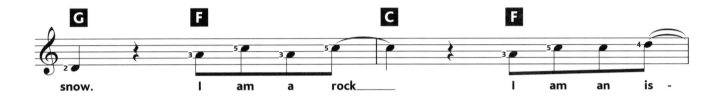

snow. I am a rock_____ I am an is -

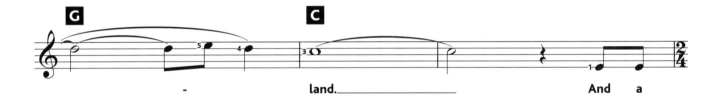

- land._____ And a

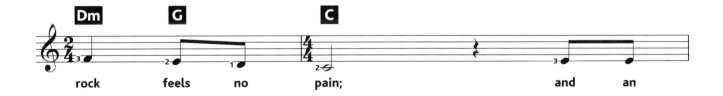

rock feels no pain; and an

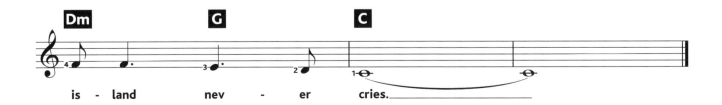

is - land nev - er cries._____

Just Give Me A Reason

Words & Music by Alecia Moore, Jeff Bhasker & Nate Ruess

Things you nev - er say to me, oh oh. Tell me that you've had e -

- nough of our love, our love.

Just give me a rea - son just a lit - tle bit's e - nough, just a

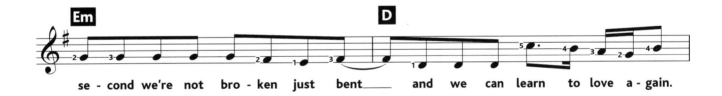

se - cond we're not bro - ken just bent____ and we can learn to love a - gain.

It's in the stars, it's been writ - ten in the scars on our hearts.

We're not bro - ken just bent____ and we can learn to love a - gain.

Knockin' On Heaven's Door

Words & Music by Bob Dylan

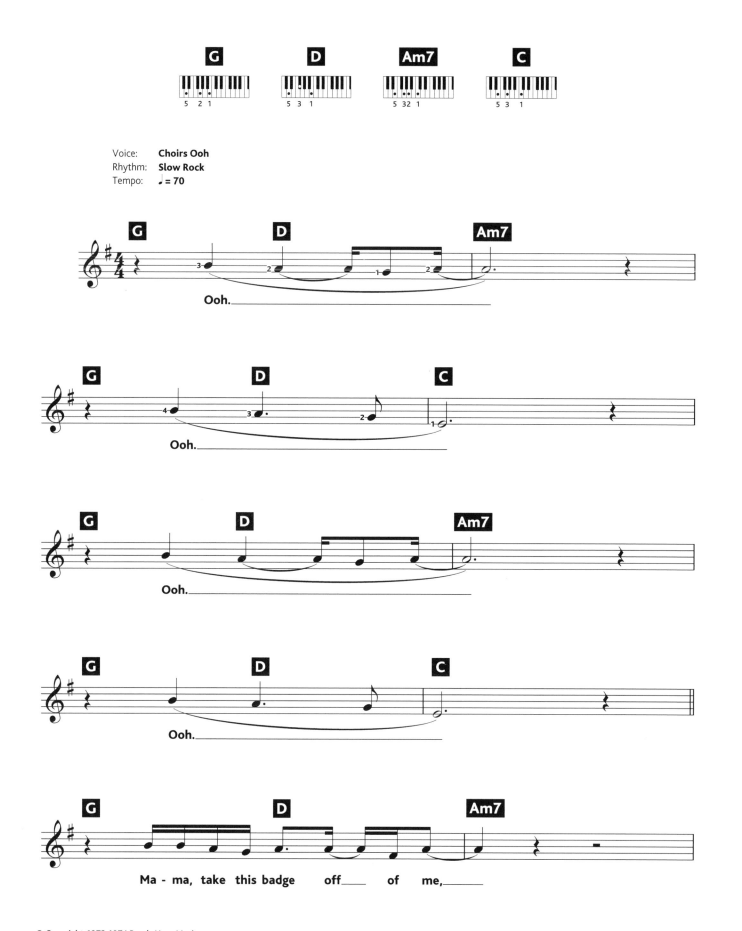

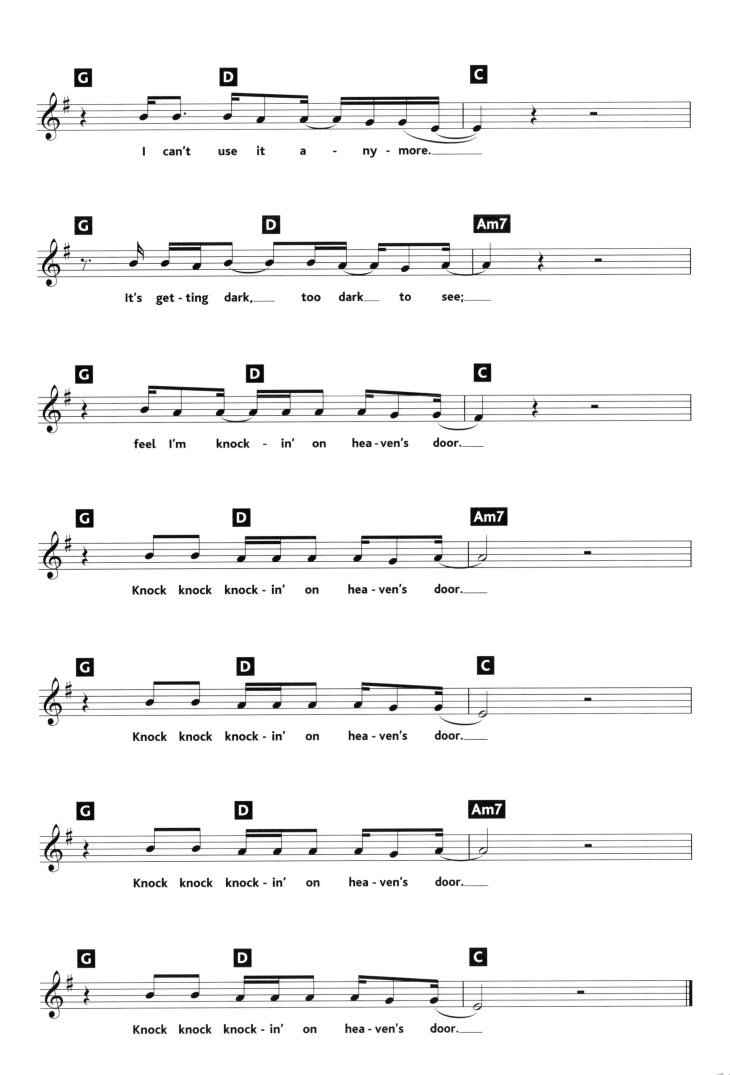

19

Mamma Mia

Words & Music by Benny Andersson, Stig Anderson & Björn Ulvaeus

Voice: **Alto Saxophone**
Rhythm: **Disco Pop**
Tempo: ♩ = 140

I've been cheat-ed by you___ since I don't know when,___

so I made up my mind___ it must come to an end.___

Look at me now,___ will I ev-er learn? I don't know how,___ but I sud-den-ly lose___

___ con - trol,___ there's a fire___ with-in___ my soul.___ Just one

look and I can hear a bell ring.___ One more look and I for-get ev-'ry-thing, oh,___ oh.___

Mam-ma mi - a, here I go a - gain,__ my, my, how__ can I re-sist you?

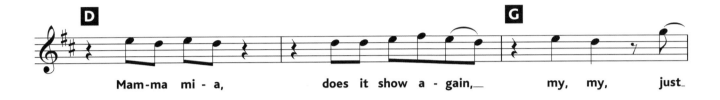

Mam-ma mi - a, does it show a - gain,__ my, my, just__

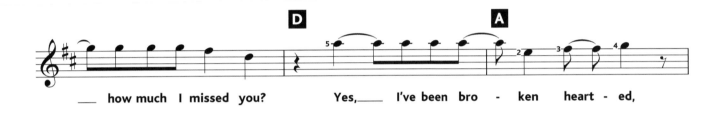

__ how much I missed you? Yes,__ I've been bro - ken heart - ed,

blue__ since the day__ we part - ed. Why, why did__

__ I ev - er let you go?__ Mam-ma mi - a, now I real - ly know,__

my, my, I__ could nev - er let you go.__

The Nearness Of You

Words by Ned Washington
Music by Hoagy Carmichael

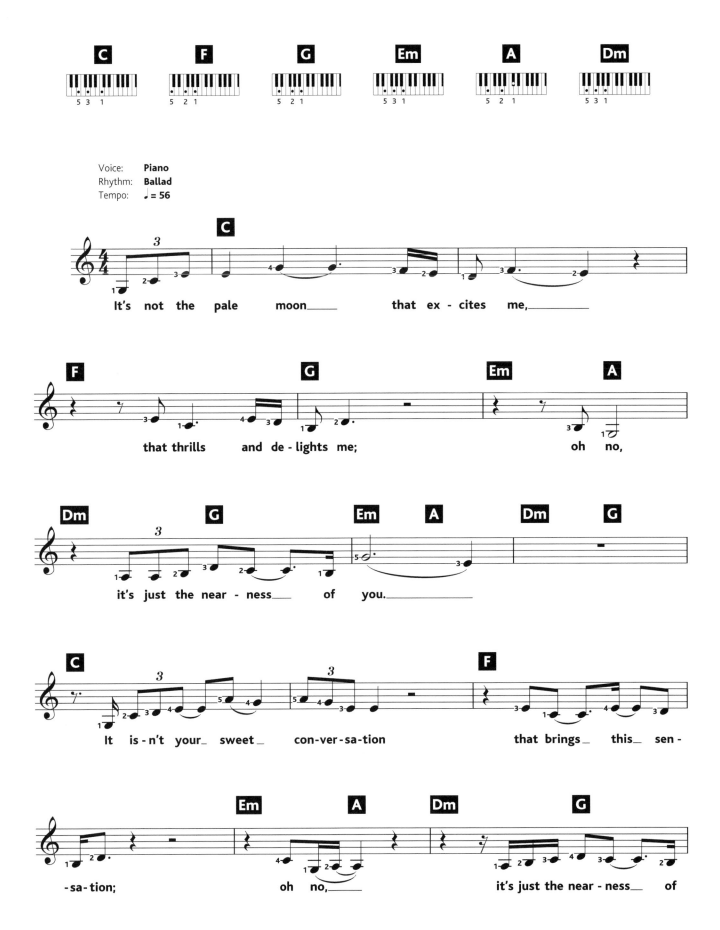

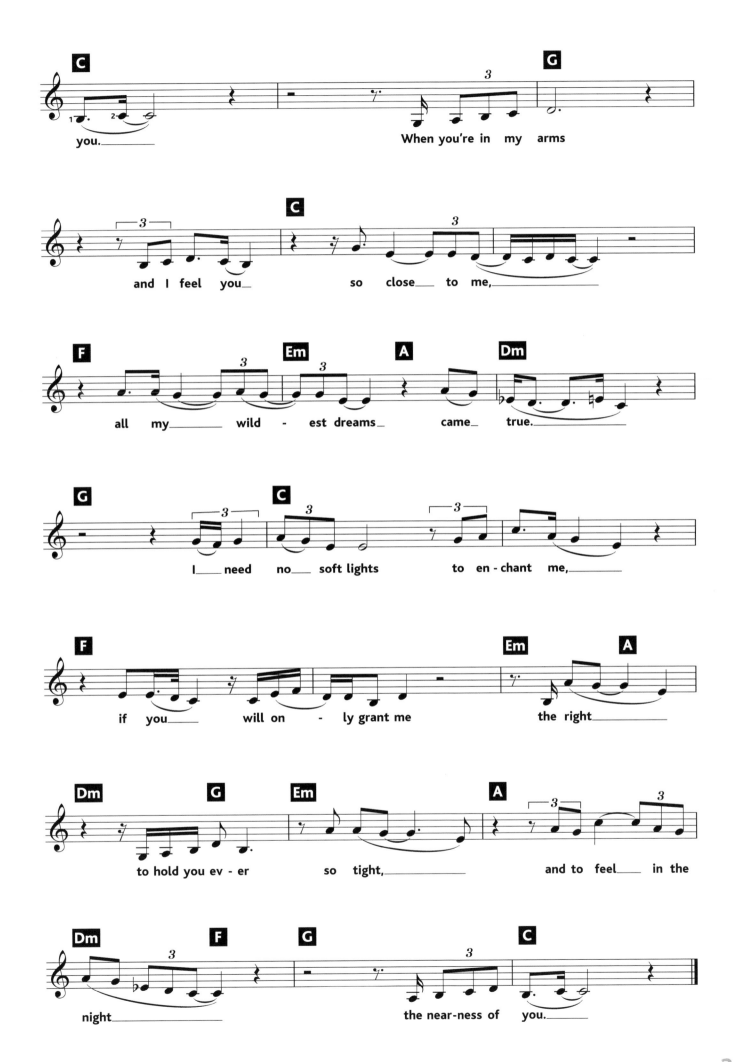

Over The Rainbow

Words by E.Y. Harburg
Music by Harold Arlen

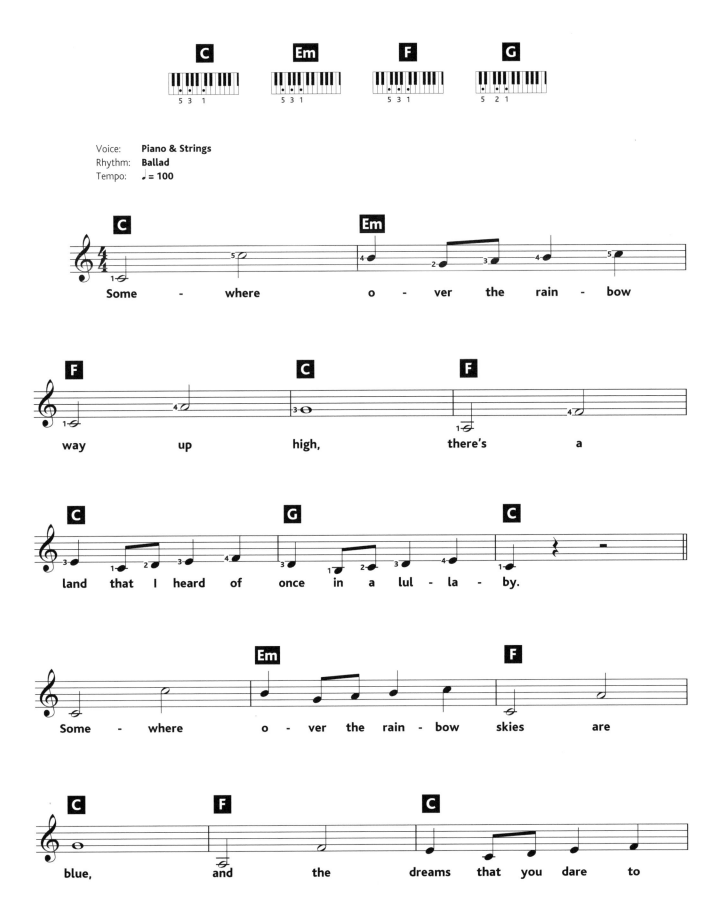

She Loves You

Words & Music by John Lennon & Paul McCartney

Voice: **Electric Guitar**
Rhythm: **Beat Rock**
Tempo: ♩ = 140

She loves you, yeah, yeah, yeah.___ She

loves you, yeah, yeah, yeah.___ She loves you, yeah,

yeah, yeah, yeah._____ You

think you've lost your love?_____ Well, I

saw her yes - ter - day._____ It's you she's think - ing of___

Shine

Words & Music by Mark Owen, Gary Barlow, Stephen Robson, Jason Orange & Howard Donald

your an - tic - i - pa - tion pulls you down,___ when you can have it all.__

___ You can have it all._____ So come on,__

___ so come on,___ get it on,___ I don't know what_ you're wait-ing for,_

___ your time is com-ing don't be late,__ hey, hey!__ So come on,_

___ see the light__ on your face,__ let it shine,_ just let it

shine,_____ let it shine.___

Smoke Gets In Your Eyes

Words by Otto Harbach
Music by Jerome Kern

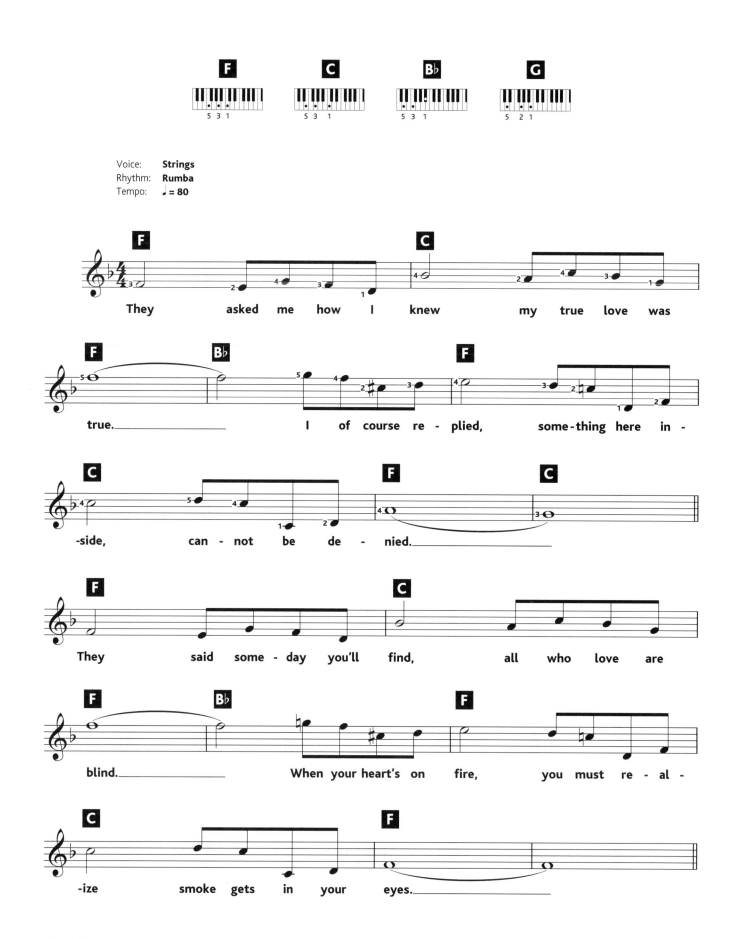

So I chaffed___ them and I gay-ly laughed___ to think they could

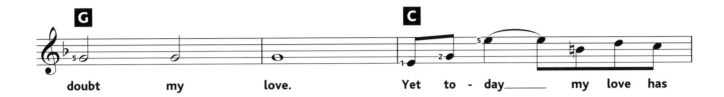

doubt my love. Yet to-day___ my love has

flown a - way,___ I am with-out my love.

Now laugh - ing friends de - ride, tears I can-not

hide,___ so I smile and say, "When a love-ly flame

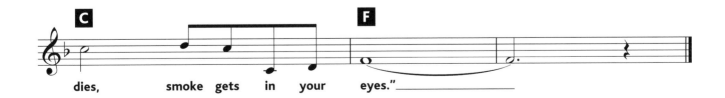

dies, smoke gets in your eyes."___

Somewhere Only We Know

Words & Music by Richard Hughes, Tim Rice-Oxley & Tom Chaplin

So tell me when___ you're gon - na let me in,___

I'm get - ting tired and I need some - where to be - gin.___

And if___ you have a min - ute why don't we go,___

talk___ a - bout it some - where on - ly we know?___

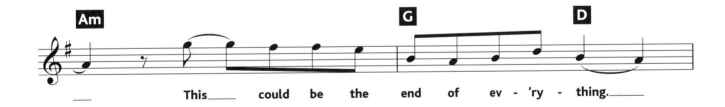

This___ could be the end of ev - 'ry - thing.___

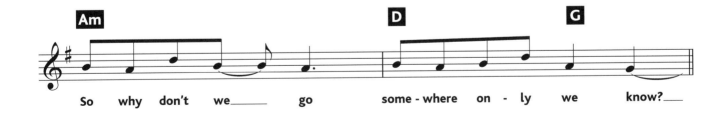

So why don't we___ go some - where on - ly we know?___

Some - where on - ly we know.___

33

(I've Had) The Time Of My Life

Words & Music by Frankie Previte, John DeNicola & Donald Markowitz

take each oth-er's hand_ 'cause we seem to un - der - stand_ the ur - gen -

- cy. Just_ re - mem - ber! You're the

one thing... I can't get e - nough_ of.

So I'll tell you some - thing,_____ This could be love. Be - cause

I've had the time of my life;_____ no, I nev -

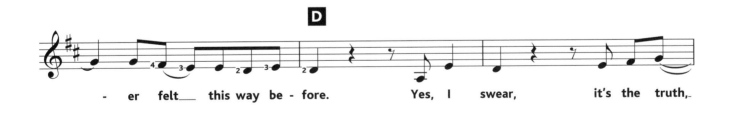

- er felt_ this way be - fore. Yes, I swear, it's the truth,_

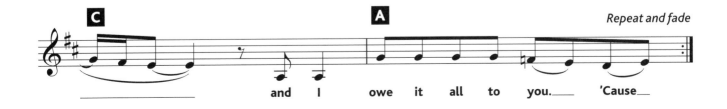

Repeat and fade

_____ and I owe it all to you._ 'Cause_

Viva La Vida

Words & Music by Guy Berryman, Jon Buckland, Will Champion & Chris Martin

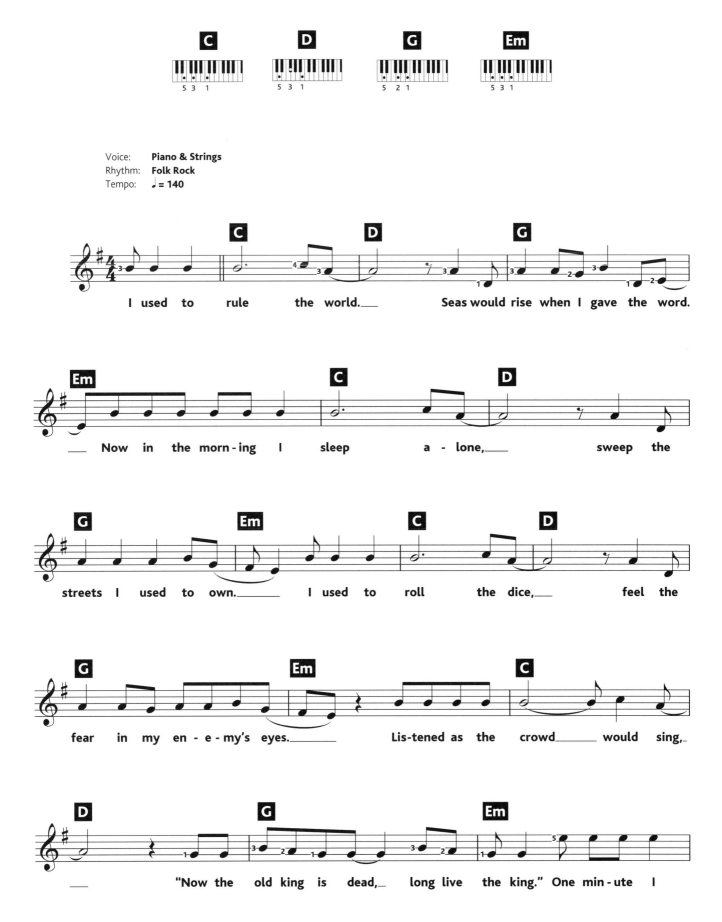

Voice: **Piano & Strings**
Rhythm: **Folk Rock**
Tempo: ♩ = 140

I used to rule the world.___ Seas would rise when I gave the word.

___ Now in the morn-ing I sleep a - lone,___ sweep the

streets I used to own.___ I used to roll the dice,___ feel the

fear in my en-e-my's eyes.___ Lis-tened as the crowd___ would sing,

___ "Now the old king is dead,___ long live the king." One min-ute I

held the key,___ next the walls were closed on me and I dis-cov-ered that my

cas - tles stand___ up-on pil-lars of salt__ and pil-lars of sand. I

hear Je - ru-sa-lem bells___ a - ring - ing. Ro - man Cav-al - ry choirs__ are sing - ing.

Be my mir-ror, my sword,_ and shield.__ My mis-sion-ar - ies in a for - eign field.___

For some rea-son I can't__ ex - plain, once you'd gone there was nev- er, nev-er an hon-

- est word,___ and that was when I ruled the world._

Repeat and fade

Your Song

Words & Music by Elton John & Bernie Taupin

Voice: **Piano**
Rhythm: **Slow Rock**
Tempo: ♩ = **64**

1. It's a lit - tle bit fun - ny,____ this feel - ing in - side.____
2. If I was a sculp - tor,____ but then a - gain no or a

I'm not one of those who can ea - si - ly hide.____
man____ who makes potions in____ the tra - velling show.____

Don't_ have much mo - ney,____ but,_ boy, if_ I did,_
I know it's not much but_____ it's the best I_ can do._

I'd buy____ big house where____ we both_ could live.
My gift__ is my song, yeah;____

this one's____ for you.____

Bringing you the words and the music

All the latest music in print... rock & pop plus jazz, blues, country, classical and the best in West End show scores.

- Books to match your favourite CDs.

- Book-and-CD titles with high quality backing tracks for you to play along to. Now you can play guitar or piano with your favourite artist... or simply sing along!

- Audition songbooks with CD backing tracks for both male and female singers for all those with stars in their eyes.

- Can't read music? No problem, you can still play all the hits with our wide range of chord songbooks.

- Check out our range of instrumental tutorial titles, taking you from novice to expert in no time at all!

- Musical show scores include *The Phantom Of The Opera*, *Les Misérables*, *Mamma Mia* and many more hit productions.

- DVD master classes featuring the techniques of top artists.